Fam
Seafood Recipes

FAMOUS *florida!*®

by Joyce LaFray

Published in the United States of America
by Seaside Publishing, Inc.

International Standard Book Number: 0-942084-36-5
Library of Congress Card Catalog Number: 87-60553

Many thanks to the restaurant owners, managers and chefs who
contributed their favorite recipes to this collection.

For additional copies write directly to:

Seaside Publishing, Inc.
P.O. Box 14441
St. Petersburg, Florida 33733-4441

A  ® Book

FLORIDA LOBSTER BISQUE

2	2 pound lobsters
1	carrot, finely chopped
1	onion, finely chopped
1	stalk celery, finely chopped
½	pound butter
2	cups white wine
2	quarts fish stock
½	teaspoon thyme
3	bay leaves
½	cup rice
12	peppercorns
1	cup tomato puree
2	cups heavy cream
1	cup brandy
	Salt and pepper to taste

Separate lobster heads from tails Cook tails in water 10 minutes. Set aside.

Saute lobster heads, carrot, onion and celery in ¼ pound butter, until lightly colored. Add wine, stock, thyme, bay leaves, rice, peppercorns, tomato puree and salt to taste. Simmer 45 minutes.

Strain bisque through fine sieve. Bring to second boil. Check seasoning. Add remaining ¼ pound butter. Add cream and brandy.

Dice meat from lobster tails. Add to bisque and serve.

Serves: 12

CATFISH CHOWDER

1½	pounds fresh water catfish
2	quarts water
¼	pound salt pork (or bacon)
2	medium onions, chopped
2	medium potatoes, diced
1	tablespoon Accent
	Tabasco Sauce to taste
	Salt and pepper to taste

Clean and wash catfish. Cook in 2 quarts of water until fish starts to come away from bone (about 15-20 minutes).

Meanwhile fry salt pork until crisp. Chop and set aside with drippings.

Carefully remove fish from bones. Return boned fish and all other ingredients to the pot.

Bring back to boil and simmer untill potatoes and onions are tender, about 10-15 minutes.

Makes: 2 quarts

SHE-CRAB SOUP

2	tablespoons finely chopped shallots
⅓	cup sherry
1½	pounds lump crab meat
3	tablespoons Hungarian paprika
2	pinches thyme
4	cups bottled clam broth
2	cups heavy cream
2	teaspoons cornstarch
½	teaspoon cayenne pepper
	Salt and fresh black pepper to taste

Combine shallots and sherry in a large saucepan and simmer until reduced by half. Add crab, paprika and thyme, and simmer for 3 minutes. Add clam broth and cream, and bring the soup to a boil.

Dissolve cornstarch in 1 teaspoon water and whisk it into the soup. Simmer for five minutes, adding seasonings to taste.

This soup tastes best made with backfin lump meat from a female crab, hence the name. The best paprika is imported from Hungary and should be stored in the freezer once opened. Fresh clam broth is best, but is available bottled.

Serves: 4-5

CONCH CHOWDER
(Made from and old Minorcan family recipe)

12	ounces conch meat or clams (well cleaned)
1/8	pound salt pork, finely chopped
2	onions, finely chopped
1	bell pepper, finely chopped
1-2	datil peppers (or hottest pepper for substitute)*
3	cups canned tomatoes, chopped
2	cups canned potatoes, diced
1/2	cup tomato puree
1/2	tablespoon thyme
1/2	tablespoon salt
1/2	tablespoon fresh ground pepper
1-2	bay leaves, crushed

Saute salt pork in large pot. Remove and set aside.
Add onions, bell pepper and saute. Add hot peppers. Add reserved salt pork and remaining ingredients.
Bring to boil 15 minutes. Simmer 45 minutes to 1 hour.

Serves: 6-8

* Datil peppers are very hot and may be difficult to find. The Ponce family has them "custom" grown for their seafood dishes. If you can't find you own datil peppers, write Surfside and we'll send you the name of a supplier.

DERBY OYSTER STEW

4	cups light cream
3	dozen fresh shucked oysters — save oyster liquor
½	cup dry white wine
2	tablespoons butter
	Salt, white pepper and caynne pepper to taste
	Fresh parsley

Poach the oysters in their own liquor and wine until their edges curl and they plump up.

Place in a double boiler. Add cream, salt, pepper and cayenne pepper. Heat until very hot.

Add butter and parsley.

Serves: 6

CONCH AND OYSTER SOUP

1	**pound conch**
1	**stick of celery**
½	**onion**
1	**pound potatoes**
8	**ounces of mushrooms**
2	**ounces butter**
2	**ounces flour**
	Pinch of thyme
	Pinch of oregano
	Pinch of ground white pepper
	Salt to taste
1½	**pints of clam juice**
12	**oysters**
	Heavy cream
	Sherry

Chop onion, mushroom, celery and conch in ¼-inch dice. Put in covered gallon saucepan with butter and herbs to sweat. Add flour to create roux and cook blonde.

Add clam juice slowly and bring to boil. Simmer 15 minutes.

Dice potatoes ¼-inch and add to soup with oysters. Cook 10 more minutes. Add salt and pepper to taste

Blend until smooth and adjust consistency with heavy cream and sherry.

Serves: 6

STONE CRABS With Mustard Sauce

5-6   **fresh stone crab claws, about 1½ pounds per person**
       Ice
       Lemon wedges
       Hot melted butter
       Mustard Sauce

Store the crabs in ice until ready to serve. To crack the claws for serving, place them on a cutting board and cover with a cloth. Crack the shell with a wide headed mallet, starting at the knuckle of the crab, working toward the claw.

Pile the prepared claws in a pyramid shape on a platter, symmetrically arranged. Garnish with lemon wedges and serve with hot melted butter and mustard sauce.

Serves: 1

Mustard Sauce

4   **ounce Coleman's English mustard**
1   **quart mayonnaise**
½   **cup A-1 sauce**
½   **cup Lea & Perrins Worcestershire**
       sauce
4   **ounce cream**

In a bowl, combine the mustard, mayonnaise, A-1 sauce and Worcestershire sauce, using a wire whisk. Beat until smooth.

Slowly add the cream and continue to beat until you reach proper sauce consistency. Sauce can be refrigerated for future.

Makes: 5 cups

9

TED PETER'S SMOKED FISH SPREAD

2	cups finely diced onion
1	cup finely diced celery
1½	cups sweet relish with pimiento
1¼	quarts Kraft Miracle Whip Salad Dressing
3½	quarts flaked smoked fish (boned), mullet preferred

Mix ingredients well. Chill. Best is served in 2-3 days.

Serves: a party

CINDY'S FISH SPREAD

1	**pound fish (flaked) from large fish carcasses or 1 pound fresh fillets (2 cups — flaked and cooked)**
1	**cup sour cream**
¼	**cup onion, chopped**
2-3	**dashes Tobasco sauce**
1-2	**dashes Worcestershire sauce**
	Lots of salt and pepper to taste
2-3	**drops Liquid Smoke**
	Crackers

Flake fish fillets or if using fish from carcasses, steam in basket over boiling water for 15 minutes until fish loosens from bones (the tastiest meat is out of the jawbones). Pick out meat.

Add sour cream to meat until spreading consistency. Add remaining ingredients. Mix well.

Spread on wafer crackers. Escort brand is an excellent choice.

You may substitute crab meat for fish.

Serves: 12-15 as an appetizer

SHRIMP MERLIN A LA FORGE

3	pounds large raw shrimp, shelled and deveined
3	quarts water
1	tablespoon thyme
½	teaspoon basil
4	hard-cooked egg yolks
4	tablespoons white wine vinegar
2-3	tablespoons sugar or more to taste
1	teaspoon dry mustard
¼	teaspoon black pepper
2½	cups mayonnaise
4	ounces capers
2	medium onions, thinly sliced
½	cup whipped cream
½	cup sour cream (whipped until smooth)
	Lettuce for garnish

Bring water to boil in a large pot. Add thyme, basil and shrimp. Bring to boil again. Reduce heat and simmer for 5 minutes or until just done and shrimp is pink. Drain and cool completely.

Press 4 egg yolks through sieve into a large bowl. Add vinegar, sugar, mustard, pepper and mayonnaise. Blend well. Add capers, onions and shrimp. Blend well again. Fold in whipped cream and sour cream. Taste for seasoning. You may wish to add more pepper and/or salt.

To serve, place in lettuce cups and garnish as you wish.

Serves: 6-8 as entree, salad or first course

BLUE LAGOON LOBSTER SALAD

2	cups cooked lobster
2	ripe pineapples
⅔	cup diced celery
½	cup macadamia nuts
¼	cup shredded coconut
⅓	cup mayonnaise
¼	cup diced kiwi fruit
	Additional kiwi for garnish

Drain and cut lobster into bit-size pieces.

Cut pineapple in half lengthwise. Remove fruit from each half and save shells.

Cut pineapple into chunks.

Combine lobster, pineapple chunks, celery, macadamia nuts, coconut, mayonnaise and kiwi fruit.

Fill the pineapple halves with mixture and garnish with sliced kiwi. (White seedless grapes can be substituted for kiwi.)

Serves: 4

CARIBBEAN CONCH SEVICHE

1	pound raw conch, finely ground
6	ounces bottled Key Lime juice
1	small cucumber
½	small red onion
½	fresh jalapeno pepper
¼	red pepper
2	tablespoons chopped parsley
3	ounces vegetable oil
22	ounces coconut milk
½	teaspoon leaf oregano
1	ounce shaved cocnut
	Dash Tabasco
1-1½	tablespoons sugar
½	tablespoon salt
	Dash ground black pepper
	Lettuce
	Bermuda onion, thinly sliced
	Alfalfa sprouts
	Cucumber and fresh basil for garnish

A day ahead: Add finely ground conch to lime juice and marinate for 24 hours.

Finely chop peppers, cucumbers, onions and parsley. Drain off excess liquid. Drain off ⅔ of the lime marinade from conch and discard. Add oil, coconut milk, seasonings and vegetables to marinated conch and mix thoroughly.

Serve on a bed of lettuce with thinly sliced bermuda onion, alfalfa sprouts, thinly sliced cucumber and a sprig of fresh basil. Garnish with a fresh Hibiscus flower.

Serves: 6

SEAGRILL'S CRAB NORFOLK

1½-2	**tablespoons butter, melted**
7-8	**ounces lump crab meat, remove cartilage**
	Salt and pepper to taste
	Accent to taste
1	**ounce white wine**

Place melted butter in a skillet in which the crab is to be served.

Add crab meat. Season with salt, pepper and Accent. Saute over medium-high heat until bubly and lightly browned. Fluff up carefully without disturbing crab lumps. Turn over and cook again until lightly brown.

As you remove skillet from the stove, quickly pour wine around the edges (may use less that 1 ounce). As it bubbles and sizzles, serve. This is a dish that will not wait.

Serves: 1

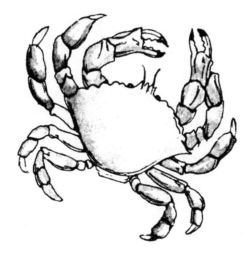

ESCABECHE DE PESCADO
(PICKLED FISH)

2	pounds red snapper fillets, cut into 12 strips
4	tablespoons flour
1	cup vegetable oil
2	pounds Bermuda onions
2	red peppers
4	chili peppers
1	cup water
2	cups white vinegar
½	teaspoon salt
1	clove garlic, peeled
½	teaspoon oregano
½	teaspoon cumin
	Salt and pepper to taste
¼	bunch fresh coriander tied with a string
3	bay leaves
3	tablespoons paprika

Dust fish fillets with 3 tablespoons flour and saute in vegetable oil. Remove from skillet with a slotted spoon and set aside.

Slice onions, red peppers and chilies into ¾-inch to 1½-inch strips, and place in sauce pan. Add water, vinegar and salt. Bring to a boil, remove from heat and stir to separate the onion and pepper strips. Strips should be crisp; do not overcook.

Saute garlic in skillet used for fish, then add all seasonings and coriander. Add remaining 1 tablespoon flour and stir well. Carefully add onions and peppers with their liquid, as oil may spatter if liquid is added too quickly.

Pour the onion mixture over the snapper, cover and refrigerate overnight.

Serve Ice Cold

Serves: 6

16

PIER HOUSE'S CONCH SALAD
(MARINATE AHEAD)

1	cucumber, peeled and seeded
1	pound conch
½	red onion
½	red pepper
½	cup cilantro (or Chinese parsley or coriander)
	Juice of 6 limes
1	cup olive oil
1	level teaspoon leaf oregano
1	level teaspoon sugar
1	level teaspoon salt
½	level teaspoon ground black pepper

Chop conch in ⅛-inch pieces, cover with lime juice. Marinate for 24 hours.

Drain. Chop onions, cucumbers, cilantro and bell pepper finely. Combine all ingredients.

Refrigerate for 24 hours.

Serves: 4

CAPTAIN BOB'S CRAB IMPERIAL

2	pounds deluxe blue crab meat (or lump crab)
2	egg yolks
1½	whole eggs
¾	cup mayonnaise
1½	teaspoons Worcestershire sauce
2	dashes Tabasco sauce
	Pinch thyme
1	teaspoon dry mustard
1½	teaspoon chopped parsley
1½	tablespoons grated Parmesan cheese (optional)

Preheat oven to 450°F.

Combine all ingredients and mix together. Portion in to individual serving dishes or place in shallow baking dish. Brush lightly with mayonnaise and sprinkle with Parmesan if desired.

Bake 10-15 minutes. Garnish with paprika and parsley.

Serves: 6-8

JOE'S SHRIMP LOUIS

1	cup fresh or frozen shrimp (70-90 per pound size)*
3-4	leaves leaf lettuce
1	cup shredded iceberg lettuce
½	tomato, quartered
1	hard-boiled egg
3-4	pitted black olives
½	cup chick peas
1	green pepper ring
	Dressing

On platter, place 3 or 4 leaves of leaf lettuce. Cover center of platter with shredded iceberg lettuce. Top with shrimp. Garnish rest of dish with the remaining ingredients. Top with Shrimp Louis Dressing.

*Also known as Titi shrimp

SHRIMP LOUIS DRESSING

1	cup mayonnaise
1½	cup chili sauce
¼	green pepper, chopped
1-2	tablespoons chopped pimiento
	Paprika
	Salt and pepper to taste
¼	teaspoon dry mustard
1	tablespoon chopped onion
	Dash Tabasco sauce
¼	teaspoon horseradish

Mix above ingredients together. Chill thoroughly.

Makes: 2½ cups.

19

STUFFED FLORIDA SWORDFISH
WITH ST. AUGUSTINE LUMP BLUE CRAB

STUFFING

2	slices bacon, chopped fine
1	tablespoon butter
2	ribs celery, diced
½	cub wild or regular white mushrooms, sliced
¼	cup diced onions
4	ounces lump blue crab meat*
1	teaspoon chopped fresh thyme
1	teaspoon chopped parsley
1	egg
2	8-ounce, thick swordfish steaks
	Salt and pepper to taste

Saute bacon in butter until golden brown. Add celery, onions and mushrooms. When nearly tender, add crab meat, salt, pepper and herbs. Remove from heat and mix in egg. Set aside to cool. Cut a pocket in swordfish and stuff with crab mixture. Grill until steaks flake easily. Serve with **CAPER BUTTER.**
*May use other varieties of crab meat.

CAPER BUTTER

¼	pound butter
2	tablespoons chopped capers
1	tablespoon chopped shallots
2	tablespoons lemon juice
1	teaspoons fresh choppped dill
1	teaspoon Dijon mustard

Soften butter at room temperature and mix with other ingredients until smooth. When swordfish is cooked, place 2 dollops of caper butter on top of each steak. Serve additional caper butter on the side.

Serves: 2

STUFFED POMPANO
A LA DINING GALLERIES

2	1½ pound pieces of pompano fillets, skinned
1	pint milk
5	ounces butter
½	ounce chopped shallots
1	clove garlic, chopped
2	ounces mushrooms, quartered
4	ounces Alaskan king crab meat
½	pint heavy cream
½	teaspoon chopped chives
	Juice of 1 lemon
	Pinch each of basil, tarragon, salt, white pepper
2	ounces flour
2	eggs, lightly beaten

Preheat oven to 350°F.

Soak fillets in milk for a few minutes. Melt 2 ounces of butter and add shallots, garlic and mushrooms and saute for 30 seconds. Stir in crab meat and cook until just heated through. Add heavy cream and chives. Simmer until thick. Season with basil, tarragon, salt, pepper and lemon juice.

Remove from stove and let cool. Sandwich mixture between 2 fillets. Dip in flour (shake off excess), then dip in egg.

Melt the remaining butter and saute the fish until brown on both sides. Put in the oven for 10-15 minutes.

Serves: 2

KON TIKI SHARK A LA SEAPORT

2	**pound shark fillets (fresh, if possible)**
	Salt to taste
	Flour for dredging
4	**eggs, beaten**
3-4	**teaspoons clarified butter**
	Coconut, shredded
½	**cup lemon juice, fresh squeezed**
	Available fresh fruit such as; peaches, apples, plums, strawberries, grapes, kiwi

Slice shark horizontally into ¼-inch thick fillets. Flatten each fillet with mallet and lightly salt. Dip into flour and then dip into egg batter.

Heat clarified butter in skillet to 400^0F. It must be very hot. Place fillets in skillet and cook until brown. Turn once and brown other side. Remove fillets from skillet and place on serving platter. Add coconut to the remaining butter in skillet.

Wash fruit and slice into ¼-inch pieces. Pat dry. Place fruit into skillet with juices. Saute very quickly. Add lemon juice to mixture. Pour sauce over fillets. Garnish and serve with potatoes and fresh vegetables.

Serves: 6-8

SHRIMP CREOLE
FROM JOE'S STONE CRAB

½	cup chopped celery
½	cup chopped onion
¼	cup chopped salt pork
1	2½ pound can tomatoes
6	ounces chili sauce
2	ounces tomato paste
½	teaspoon thyme
1	teaspoon Maggi seasoning
2	cloves garlic, finely chopped
	Salt and pepper to taste
2	pounds shrimp, peeled, deveined and cooked

Simmer celery, onions and salt pork until salt pork is cooked.

Add all the other ingredients (except shrimp) and cook for 30 minutes over a low flame.

Add shrimp and warm through.

Serve over rice.

Serves: 4-6

SNAPPER RANGOON

1	6 ounce snapper fillet
	Salt and pepper to taste
	Flour for dredging
1	egg
½	cup milk
5	tablespoons sweet (unsalted) butter
1½	ounces fresh lime juice
1	cup diced fruit (can use any one or a combination such as banana, melon, pineapple, strawberry or mango
	Chopped parsley

Dredge fish in flour that has been mixed with salt and pepper to taste. Beat egg with milk and dip fish in it.

Melt 2 tablespoons of butter. Saute the fish for a few minutes and then turn over. The amount of time depends upon the thickness of the fish. When fish is done, remove from heat and keep warm.

Melt remaining 3 tablespoons of butter. Add lime juice and fruit, and cook, swirling the parn until the fruit is heated through. The juices will thicken on their own.

Pour the juices over the fish and sprinkle with chopped parsley.

Serves: 1

CRAB POT'S FAMOUS CRAB CAKES

4	pounds crab meat, shredded
1	pound crab meat, lump
5	eggs
30	crushed crackers
1	cup mayonnaise
5	tablespoons Worcestershire sauce
	Fresh parsley, chopped
1	cup prepared mustard
	Salt
5	tablespoons Old Bay seasoning
	Vegetable oil for frying

Preheat oven to 200^0F.

Pick over crab meat very carefully to remove shells and cartilage. Beat eggs.

Spread the 4 pounds shredded crab meat evenly in a flat pan. Add crackers, mayonnaise, eggs, Worcestershire sauce, parsley, mustard, salt and the seasonings. Mix well with your hands.

Add the lump crab meat. Shuffle into the mixture gently. Form into 30 cakes and dust with flour.

Fry at about 350^0F for about 3 minutes on each side until golden brown. Keep warm in the oven.

Serves: 8-10

CONCH FRITTERS
from The Vilano Seafood Shack

2	cups self-rising flour
2	cups conch, tenderized and finely chopped
1	large onion, diced
1	green pepper, diced
	Salt and pepper
2	dashes Tabasco sauce
2	eggs, lightly beaten
¾	cup milk (approximately)

Combine all of the above ingredients with enough milk for the mixture to hold its shape

Form into fritters and fry in 350°F oil until golden.

Drain on paper towels and serve with the sauce below (or the sauce of your choice).

HOT SAUCE

24	ounces catsup
¼	cup Worcestershire sauce
3	datil (or very hot peppers), finely chopped

Combine all of the ingredients. Makes 1 quart and will keep in a covered glass jar for a week or two.

Serves: 4-6

SHRIMP SUZANNE WITH DILL

1	pound (25-30 count) shrimp, cooked, peeled and cleaned
½	cup sour cream
½	cup mayonnaise
½	cup cucumber soup of ½ fresh cucumber, seeded and scraped with spoon
⅓	cup finely chopped onions
1½	tablespoons fresh chopped dill
1½	teaspoons lemon juice
½	teaspoon garlic salt
¼	teaspoon fresh ground pepper
¼	teapoon or 8 drops Tabasco sauce
¼	teaspoon caraway seed

Mix ingredients well. Chill well.
Serve on a bed of Bibb lettuce, either as individual servings or in lettuce-lined bowls.

Serves: 4-6

MAI-KAI'S SCALLOPS SINGAPORE

2	tablespoons peanut oil
¼	teaspoon salt
¼	teaspoon Accent
10	ounces bay scallops
1"	sliced ginger, peeled, smashed and chopped
8	large mushrooms, sliced in thirds
½	tablespoon sherry
½	cup chicken broth
1	scallion, trimmed and shredded
1	tablespoon Oriental oyster sauce (Available in groceries or import food stores, you may substitute soy sauce.)
1	tablespoon cornstarch

Heat peanut oil in a wok or large skillet over medium-high heat. Add salt and Accent.

Add scallops and ginger and stir briefly. Add mushrooms and sherry.

Stir constantly while adding chicken broth, oyster sauce and scallion. Stir and gradually add cornstarch until sauce starts to thicken. Serve immediately.

Serves: 2

CAPTAIN BILL'S SNAPPER FILLETS

4	snapper fillets
2	tomatoes, pelled and thinly sliced
	Seasoned bread crumbs
	Salt and pepper
½	cup white wine
½	stick (¼ cup) butter
1	teaspoon lemon or lime juice
	Parmesan cheese, grated
	Paprika

Preheat oven to 500°F.

Arrange 1 layer of the sliced tomatoes in individual or 1 large baking dish. Sprinkle each dish with 3 tablespoons seasoned bread crumbs and season with salt and pepper. Overlap small snapper fillets over tomatoes.

In a saucepan, combine wine, butter and lemon juice. Cook this mixture over low heat until butter is melted. Increase the heat to moderate. Boil the mixture for 1-2 minutes.

Divide the mixture among the fillets and sprinkle each serving with 2 tablespoons freshly grated Parmesan cheese and paprika to taste.

Bake the fish in oven for 10 minutes.

Serves: 4

SHRIMP CREPES A LA FORGE

1	pound cooked shrimp, cut into ¼-inch chunks, set aside
3	tablespoons butter
1	tomato, finely chopped
1	clove garlic, mashed
3	shallots, minced (or scallions)
1	tablespoon chicken broth powder
1	teaspoon thyme
⅛	teaspoon oregano
	Salt and pepper to taste
1	cup Bechamel sauce
1	cup heavy cream
2	tablespoons bourbon
½	cup Gruyere or Swiss cheese grated
2	tablespoons parsley, minced
½	tablespoon paprika

Preheat oven to 375°F.

In a large skillet heat butter. Add tomato, garlic and shallots. Add powdered chicken broth, seasonings, bechamel and cream. Cook for 2-3 minutes. Add bourbon and cheese and simmer until cheese is melted.

Combine ½ of the sauce with the shrimp. Place shrimp mixture onone half of the crepe. Fold over the crepe forming a semi-circle.

Place crepes into a well buttered baking pan and heat at 375°F for 5-6 minutes. Serve crepes with 2-3 tablespoons of the remaining sauce over each crepe, sprinkled with parsley and paprika.

BECHAMEL SAUCE

1½	tablespoons butter
1½	tablespoons flour
1	cup milk
	Salt and pepper to taste

In a saucepan melt butter. Add flour and stir well. Add mild and seasonings and whisk with a wire whip. Simmer, whisking continuously until consistency of thick cream.

Makes: 12

GROUPER w/MANGO & PEACH SAUCE

1	**4-6 pound grouper**
¼	**cup flour**
⅓	**cup vegetable oil**
	Lemon and fresh parsley for garnish
	Hot sauce

Preheat oven to 375°F.

Dust the grouper with flour on both sides. Heat oil in large heavy skillet and saute fish until golden brown, about 5 minutes per side.

Place on a heat-proof platter in the oven to finish cooking, for about 7-10 minutes, depending on the thickness of the fish. Do not overcook the fish, it should remain moist.

Place fish on a serving platter and top with the hot sauce.
Garnish with lemon and parsley.

HOT SAUCE

6	**ounces fresh mango, pitted and peeled (about 1 large)**
6	**ounces fresh peaches, pitted and peeled (about 3 medium)**
2	**ounces melon flavored liqueur**

Puree mango and peaches in a blender or food processor. Place in a saucepan and bring to a boil. Stir in the melon liqueur, then reduce heat to low to keep sauce warm until ready to serve.

Serves: 2

FISH RANGOON

2	pounds of fillets of yellowtail, snapper, grouper or similar firm white fish, with all bones and skin removed
1	teaspoon Worcestershire sauce
2	tablespoons fresh lemon juice
1	teaspoon salt
¼	teaspoon white pepper
	Flour for dredging
	Egg wash (2 eggs with a little milk)
½	cup clarified oleo or vegetable oil
¼	teaspoon ground cinnamon
3	tablespoons currant jelly
	Rangoon sauce

Season fillets with Worcestershire sauce, lemon juice, salt and pepper. Dip fillets in flour, then the egg wash.

Meanwhile, heat the oleo or oil in a heavy skillet. Place the fillets in the skillet. Saute until light brown. Turn fillet over and continue saute until fish is cooked — just a few minutes. When fillets are done, place on a serving platter. Sprinkle with ground cinnamon and spread currant jelly over them. Keep warm. Discard oleo or oil and wipe out the skillet. Top each serving of fish with some of the Rangoon sauce and serve.

RANGOON SAUCE

½	cup each of diced bananas, pineapple, mangoes and papayas (may substitute peaches if mangoes or papyas are not available)
2	sticks butter (8 ounces)
1	tablespoon fresh chopped parsley
2	tablespoons fresh lemon juice

Use skillet that you prepared the fish in. Melt butter, add fruit, parsley and lemon juice. Shake skillet until heated through. Be careful not to cook or heat too long.

Serves: 4

SHRIMP ALMENDRINA
WITH ORANGE MUSTARD SAUCE

2	eggs
2	cups milk
2	cups flour
	Salt and fresh ground pepper
2½	pounds jumbo shrimp, peeled and deveined, tails left intact
4	cups sliced almonds
	Oil for deep frying
	Orange mustard sauce

Beat eggs until light and fluffy in a medium bowl. Stir in milk. Gradually mix in flour, blending well. Add salt and pepper to taste.

Holding the shrimp by tail, dip into batter, allowing excess to drip back into the bowl. Do not cover tails with batter. Sprinkle all sides of batter coated shrimp with almonds. Place on cookie sheet and refrigerate at least 2 hours before frying.

Heat oil to 375°F. Deep fry shrimp a few at a time, just until they turn pink, about 2 minutes. Do not overcook. Drain on paper towels and keep warm until all shrimp have been cooked. Serve immediately with Orange Mustard Sauce.

ORANGE MUSTARD SAUCE

¾	cup sweet orange marmalade
¼	cup chicken or beef stock
2	tablespoons fresh lemon juice
1	teaspoon dry mustard
	Few drops hot pepper sauce

Thoroughly combine all ingredients. Makes about 1 cup.

Serves: 6-8

MUCKY DUCK'S CHARCOAL GRILLED SWORDFISH WITH FRUIT SALSA

SALSA:

1/4	cup diced kiwi
1/4	cup diced pineapple
1/4	cup diced cantaloupe, or honey dew melon
1/3	cup diced red bell pepper
1/4	cup diced yellow bell pepper
10	slices Greek peppers*, 2 tablespoons juice reserved
2	tablespoons juice from Greek peppers
2	tablespoons pineapple juice
1	teaspoon chili powder
1	teaspoon ground cumin

FISH:

1/4	cup melted sweet unsalted butter
6	6-ounce swordfish fillets
	Seasoned salt to taste
4-6	cups cooked long grain white rice

Prepare salsa first, by mixing together all the salsa ingredients in a large non-metallic bowl. Cover and refrigerate for at least 3 hours.

With a pastry brush, butter the fish and add the seasoned salt. Cook the fillets on a charcoal grill for 3-5 minutes per side, depending on the thickness of the filets.

For each serving, place a bedding of long grain white rice in the middle of an attractive plate. Place a portion of the fish, then spoon the fruit salsa on top of each fillet.

**or 2 jalapeños, cored, seeded and diced

Serves: 4-6

PERRY'S SEAFOOD HOUSE BAKED FISH FILLETS

2-4	garlic cloves, crushed
3/4	cup olive oil
	Juice of 1 lemon
1	10 ounce fillet of grouper
	Chopped parsley for garnish
	Lemon wedges for garnish

Preheat oven to 400 degrees F. In a small bowl, mix the crushed garlic cloves together with the olive oil and lemon juice. Rub each fillet with a liberal amount of the mixture, then bake for about 15-20 minutes, or until just done. Do not overcook. Pour the remaining oil mixture over the fillets.

Serve hot with chopped parsley and lemon wedges for garnish.

Serves: 4

PERRY'S FAMOUS COCKTAIL SAUCE

2	cups chili sauce
4	tablespoons Worcestershire sauce
2	cups ketchup
2	teaspoons dry mustard, such as Coleman's
2	teaspoons salt to taste
4	tablespoons creamed horseradish
3	teaspoons fresh ground black pepper
	Juice of 1 lemon

In a very large non-metallic bowl mix together chili sauce, Worcestershire, ketchup, mustard, salt, horseradish, black pepper and fresh lemon juice. Combine well, refrigerate until ready to use.

Serve with oysters, scallops, shrimp or other seafood. Store refrigerated.

Makes: About 4 1/2 cups

FRESH CONCH AND LOBSTER CEVICHE

SEAFOOD:

2	cups diced conch
2	cups poached and diced lobster

VEGETABLES:

1/4	cup diced Bermuda onion
1/4	cup diced red bell pepper
1/4	cup fresh corn, kernels separated
1/4	cup peeled and diced papaya
1/8	cup fresh lime juice
1/4	cup rice wine vinegar
1/2	cup extra virgin olive oil
1	teaspoon fresh chopped jalapeño peppers*
1	tablespoon honey
2	tablespoons chopped cilantro leaves
2	tablespoons chopped fresh basil
2	tablespoons chopped mint leaves
1/4	cup chopped scallions
	Salt and pepper to taste
	Leafy greens and sliced bell peppers for garnishing

Wash and clean seafood well. In a medium size glass bowl combine seafood, then the vegetables. Toss well. Add more seasoning according to taste, then marinate in the refrigerator for 3-5 hours, tossing occasionally to mix. Just before serving adjust seasonings.

Serve on a large bed of leafy greens with colorful bell pepper garnish.

*or other hot pepper, seeds removed

Serves: 8-10

KEY LARGO BAY
SCALLOPS SEVICHE

2	cups bay scallops
1/3	cup Key Lime juice*
1/3	cup green, red, and yellow peppers, finely diced & combined
2	scallions, trimmed and diced
1	tomato, diced
1	teaspoon fresh chopped dill
	Leafy greens for bedding

Place scallops, juice, bell peppers, scallions, tomato and dill into a large bowl. Toss gently, then place in refrigerator to marinate for at least one hour. Serve on a bed of leafy greens.

*May substitute regular lime juice

Serves: 4

KEY WEST SHRIMP IN SAUCE CALYPSO

1 pound medium shrimp (25-30), shelled and deveined

SAUCE:

1	cup mayonnaise
1/3	cup ketchup
1/3	cup whipped heavy cream
1	ounce good brandy
	Tabasco to taste
1	head iceberg lettuce
1	lemon cut into 4 wedges

Rinse shrimp well and drain.

Prepare sauce in a medium size bowl by gently folding in mayonnaise, ketchup, heavy cream, brandy and Tabasco to taste.

Blend well.

Serve on a bed of lettuce. Garnish with lemon wedges.

Serves: 4

CRAB PUFFS A LA MUCKY DUCK

1	pound lump crab claw meat, picked over
1	teaspoon butter or margarine
1/4	cup minced onion
1/4	cup minced green bell pepper
1/4	cup minced celery
1/4	cup Sherry wine
1/2	cup toasted bread crumbs
1	egg, slightly beaten
1/8	teaspoon dry mustard, such as Coleman's
1/8	teaspoon ground red pepper
1/8	teaspoon Old Bay Seasoning
1/3	cup mayonnaise
	Vegetable oil for deep frying
	Cocktail sauce or Dijon mustard sauce

Melt the butter or margarine in a large skillet that has been heated to medium hot. Add in the onion, bell pepper, and celery and cook until just crisp. Pour in Sherry, then cook about two more minutes. Remove pan from heat and set aside to cool.

In a large bowl, mix together the lump crab meat, half of the bread crumbs, egg, mustard, red pepper, Old Bay and mayonnaise. Add in the vegetable mix and blend thoroughly, then, using cleaned hands, roll into 2-ounce balls. If the mixture is too sticky, add more crumbs. If too dry, add a bit more mayonnaise. Roll the balls in the rest of the crumbs. Heat the oil for deep frying and when hot, drop in the puffs and fry for 3-5 minutes, or until golden.

Serve with a good cocktail or Dijon mustard sauce.

Serves: 4

SHRIMP SCAMPI EXCELLENCE

2	pounds jumbo shrimp, shelled, deveined and butterflied
1/4	pound butter (1 stick)
1/2	cup olive oil
1/2	cup scallions
1	garlic clove, finely chopped
1	teaspoon lemon or lime juice
	Salt and pepper to taste
2	tablespoons parsley, finely chopped
3	lemons, quartered

Preheat broiler.

Wash shrimp well under cold water. Melt butter in a saucepan over low heat, then stir in olive oil, lemon or lime juice, scallions, garlic and salt and pepper to taste.

Place shrimp in a 13" x 9" x 2" baking pan in one layer. Use another pan if necessary. Pour melted mixture over shrimp, then turn shrimp over, making sure to cover on both sides. Broil 4 inches from the heat for about 6 minutes. Turn over and broil for another 6 minutes, or until shrimp are lightly browned but not overcooked.

Place shrimp on heated plates. Pour sauce from broiler pan over shrimp. Sprinkle with parsley and serve with fresh lemon quarters.

Serves:　4

SCALLOPS DES CARAIBES

3	tablespoons butter or margarine
1	pound bay or sea scallops, washed and drained
2	tablespoons vegetable oil
2	tablespoons overproof (151%) rum
1	tablespoon mild curry powder
3	tablespoons mango chutney
1/2	cup heavy cream
1	tablespoon unsalted butter, melted
	Salt and freshly ground black pepper to taste

In a large non-stick skillet, heat butter or margarine until melted and sizzling. Add scallops and stir gently with a wooden spoon for about 2 minutes. Transfer scallops to plate. Cover and keep warm.

Discard the remaining butter from skillet and place over low heat. Carefully pour the rum into the skillet and carefully flambé. Add curry, chutney and heavy cream. Cook for about 1 minute, then add butter, a and combine well. Add scallops, heat through, but be careful not to boil or overcook.

Season to taste with salt and pepper. Serve over rice or as an appetizer with a portion of sauce for dipping.

Serves: 4

HENRY'S SAUTEED YELLOWTAIL
WITH CHARDONNAY BUTTER SAUCE

8	4-ounce yellowtail fillets
1/3	cup clarified butter
2	cups all-purpose flour
1/2	Chardonnay wine
4	leaves fresh sorrel* or basil leaves
1	tomato, blanched, seeded and diced
1/2	cup butter or margarine
	Salt and pepper to taste
1	lemon cut into 4 wedges
	Parsley sprigs for garnish

Pour clarified butter into a large skillet that has been heated to medium high. Dip fillets into flour, then sauté until golden brown on one side. Flip over and brown other side. Cook until done.

In a medium size saucepan simmer the Chardonnay until reduced to 1/4 of the original volume, then add butter and swirl in pan. Add salt and pepper to taste.

Roll sorrel or basil leaves and cut lengthwise into thin ribbons. For presentation place 1 fillet each plate, then add some of the diced tomato and a few sorrel or basil ribbons. Place another fillet directly on top and spoon the Chardonnay sauce on top over all.

Garnish with a lemon wedges and sprigs of parsley

*Available at most Caribbean stores, especially Jamaican.

Serves: 4

KEY WEST SHRIMP AMAROUSE

3 - 4	tablespoons olive oil
4	tablespoons minced garlic
4	tablespoons finely chopped basil
20	medium size shrimp
1	cup shredded carrots
8	large mushrooms, quartered
2	ounces Pernod liqueur
2	ounces dry white wine
8	tablespoons unsalted butter or margarine
8	tablespoons blanched, slivered almonds
4	teaspoons chopped parsley

Heat oil in a large sauté pan over medium heat. Add the garlic, basil and shrimp, then sauté until shrimp turns white and is cooked, but not overdone.

Add in carrots and mushrooms, then pour in Pernod and carefully flambé. Pour in white wine, then add in butter and swirl the pan until butter becomes liquid. Stir in almonds, then remove from heat.

Arrange a mound of the carrot and mushrooms in the center of 4 plates. Carefully place 5 shrimp around vegetables on each plate. Pour sauce over all. Garnish with chopped parsley.

Serves: 4

— *Notes* —

re-order information

Copy this form and send to:

Publishing, Inc.
P.O. Box 14441
St. Petersburg, Florida 33733-4441

Please send me _____copies of **Famous Florida!® Seafood Recipes** at $5.95 per copy. Add $3.50 for postage and handling for the first book ordered and .50 for each additional copy. Make check payable to *Seaside Publishing*.

Name _____

Street _____

City _____

State & Zip _____

1-888-FLA-BOOK (352-2665)

— *Notes* —

re-order information

Copy this form and send to:

Seaside
Publishing, Inc.
P.O. Box 14441
St. Petersburg, Florida 33733-4441

Please send me _____copies of **Famous Florida!**® **Seafood Recipes** at $5.95 per copy. Add $3.50 for postage and handling for the first book ordered and .50 for each additional copy. Make check payable to

Seaside
Publishing, Inc.

Name _____

Street _____

City _____

State & Zip _____

888-FLA-BOOK (352-2665)

— Notes —